ONE EARTH

WHERE ARE MY BEARS?

RON HIRSCHI

Photographs by ERWIN and PEGGY BAUER

National
Audubon
Society

 BANTAM BOOKS · NEW YORK · TORONTO · LONDON · SYDNEY · AUCKLAND

With thanks
to Diane, Martha, and Nancy

If you would like to receive more
information about the National Audubon Society write to:
National Audubon Society, Membership Department,
950 Third Avenue, New York, NY 10022

WHERE ARE MY BEARS?
A Bantam Book / October 1992

Executive Editor: Christopher N. Palmer

Library of Congress Cataloging-in-Publication Data

Hirschi, Ron.
   Where are my bears? / Ron Hirschi : photographs by Erwin and Peggy Bauer.
     p.   cm.—(One Earth)
  "A National Audubon Society book."
  Summary: Describes the lifestyle and habitat of the grizzly bear, how the destruction of forest land threatens its survival, and
what we can do to save the grizzly.
   ISBN 0-553-07805-4.—ISBN 0-553-35473-6 (pbk.)
   1. Grizzly bear—Juvenile literature. 2. Endangered species—United States—Juvenile literature. [1. Grizzly bear. 2. Bears. 3.
Rare animals. 4. Wildlife conservation.] I. Bauer, Erwin A., ill. II. Bauer, Peggy, ill. III. Title. IV. Series: Hirschi, Ron. One Earth.
QL737.C27H56   1992
599.74'446—dc20   91-13405 CIP AC

ABOUT THE ONE EARTH BOOKS

During its nearly one hundred years of educating the public about environmental issues, the National Audubon Society has rarely achieved anything as important as reaching out to the world's young people, the voices of tomorrow. For Audubon and its 600,000 members, nothing is so crucial as ensuring that those voices speak in the future on behalf of wildlife.

Audubon reaches out to people in many ways—through its nationwide system of wildlife sanctuaries, through research vital to helping set the nation's environmental policy, through lobbying for sound conservation laws, through television documentaries and fact-based dramatic films, through *Audubon* magazine and computer software, and through ecology workshops for adults and Audubon Adventures clubs in school classrooms. Each of these is critical to reaching a large audience. And now, with the Audubon One Earth books, the environmental community can speak to the youngest minds in our citizenry.

Audubon is proud to publish One Earth in cooperation with Bantam Books. In addition to bringing new information and experiences to young readers, these books will instill in them a fundamental concern for the environment and its decline at the hands of humanity. They will also, it is hoped, stimulate an undying interest in the natural world that will empower young people, as they mature, to protect the world's natural wonders for themselves and for future generations.

We at Audubon hope you will enjoy the One Earth books and that you will find in them an inspiration for joining our earth-saving mission. Young people are the hope for our future.

Christopher N. Palmer
Executive Editor
President, National Audubon
Society Productions

INTRODUCTION

Mountains and forests stretch across the land. But we have broken these forests into smaller and smaller islands of trees. Often these patches of forest are too small to meet the needs of many animals. Even the ancient forests, which were once filled with life, have been replaced by crops of trees cut too soon in their lives to support plants and animals needing shady hideaways, rich layers of moss, or the shelter of an old fallen log.

The loss of grizzly bears is one of the most striking examples of how thoroughly we have destroyed our environment. Needing true wilderness, grizzlies will survive only if we give them land all their own. Join us now as we travel from the places where many of us live in comfort to the Rocky Mountains and northwestern forests of the United States where grizzly bears need our help to save their last homes.

Come walk with me to the city park where squirrels jump from branch to branch, search for acorns in golden leaves, and run up trees if we walk too close.

Chickadees sing from their perch in the squirrel's favorite oak. Robins nest close to the houses where they find plenty of worms.

But where are my bears? They once lived
here, too.

Out in the meadow, chipmunks scurry through tangles of twigs. Rabbits munch clover and run for cover if danger comes too near.

In the shelter of trees, raccoons chase frogs at the streambank and sleep in an old fallen log.

A family of foxes or a striped skunk might live nearby.

But what about bears?

Grizzlies might have lived here until people came with their guns, bulldozers, buildings, and roads.

Now grizzlies are in danger and live in faraway woods.

Out in the country, farm fields cover the land. Deer nibble tender sprouts and tree buds. They leap through fields and hide in what little is left of the tall oak woods.

But where can bears hide? Where can they roam free?

In the forest where trees grow wilder still, deer are much safer. A doe can hide her spotted fawn.

Foxes and
coyotes can
hunt for

a breakfast
of mice . . .

where
woodpeckers,

cardinals,
owls,

and bobcats
find homes.

Can you hear the growl
of black bears? Can they live
in these wild woods, too?

If they find plenty of berries, ants, honey, nuts, and other food. And if they find enough trees.

Even where we build our houses—if black bears can still find safe places to sleep through the winter and food for their families—the forests can be home for these furry tree climbers. But what about grizzlies, those mighty brown bears?

Once grizzly bears found homes on the Great Plains, in California, and throughout all of the Rocky Mountains. Then people shot and killed them, built too many roads into the grizzlies' mountains, and changed the grizzlies' homeland into a land of cows and sheep. Now grizzlies are endangered and need all our help.

The last of the grizzlies south of Canada live high in the mountains, far from human towns.

They live where cougars can still raise their kittens, and in the wildest of wolverine woods.

Grizzly bears live where bald eagles soar over rivers filled with salmon that leap swift waterfalls. You might hike here and visit for a while. But grizzlies need land without people. Theirs is not a home for you or for me.

Grizzly bears follow elk or caribou herds in springtime. And when the snowy season

draws near, they need plenty of pine nuts to be ready for hibernation, their long winter nap.

Grizzlies need so much land, their homes stretch farther than you can see. They need room to roam, room to run free.

Grizzly bears
play with their babies,
munch grass like
bunnies,

and catch fish
with their paws.

Grizzlies are swift as wild horses. Grizzlies are strong. But the great grizzly bears are disappearing.

Only you can save them and their special home.

Afterword

For young readers, parents, teachers,
big brothers, and big sisters:

Once, grizzly bears roamed the forests and grasslands of California—even to the edge of the San Francisco Bay. They were so much a part of that state that they were made its symbol. Now the grizzly is only a memory in those and many other hills that roll across America. Today grizzlies are mainly found in Montana, Wyoming, Idaho, Alaska, and parts of Canada.

But grizzly bears are only one of the many animals that once thrived in the midst of Native American people who hunted the same prey as the great bears, who walked the same mountains, and who respected the balances in nature.

Wild animals have not disappeared simply because we take up so much more room. They disappear because we fail to ensure that their needs are met and because we kill them. Even today, grizzly bears, wolves, and eagles are shot by ranchers and others who feel their livelihood is threatened by these vanishing species.

Can animals like the grizzly bear remain safe from extinction when they are continually threatened by the ever-increasing levels of human activity?

Perhaps the ability of black bears to survive in Pennsylvania, the outskirts of Seattle, and in the Michigan woods offers some insight into how we can save other animals and wild landscapes. Black bears can thrive near humans when forested areas are extensive enough to provide the basic needs of food, shelter, and secure places for rearing cubs. If we protect existing forests and begin to restore former forestland, many animals will find homes for the future. This restoration can begin with a single seed. With your nurturing, that seed can grow into a healthier future . . . and if it takes firm root, maybe someday a grizzly bear will hibernate within the tangle of protective trees you have planted.

ACTIVITIES

Things you can do to help save grizzly bears and other wildlife of mountains, forests, and wilderness lands:

- Plant a tree each month in a place where forests once grew, making sure it is native to that area.

- As a family or school project, adopt a local forest, helping to protect it from destruction. The National Audubon Society can help you learn how.

- Use recycled paper products to help save forests. And reuse paper products, too.

- As a school project, adopt grizzly bears, cougars, or wolves as special animals to study and to protect. Contact a zoo near you to find out how their adoption programs work.

- Avoid disturbing wildlife homes, especially in springtime.

- Visit a local forested park or other neighborhood woodland, getting to know some of the animals living where trees and old fallen logs offer them a home.

- Visit Yellowstone and Glacier national parks to learn more about grizzly bears and their special needs.

- As a school or family project, write letters to your congressional representatives, urging them to make sure grizzly bear needs are met before our national parks and forests are changed in ways that harm bear feeding grounds or other special areas.

- As a family, school, or community project, begin to identify and protect local areas that offer homes for wildlife you enjoy and love.

About the Author

Ron Hirschi is a renowned environmentalist who worked as a habitat biologist before turning full time to writing and working with children. He now visits children in classrooms and communities nationwide, inspiring their curiosity and helping them to see that there are many things they can do in their own backyards to make our earth a better place.

Ron has written twenty books for children, including the acclaimed *Winter* and *Spring* books and the recently published Discover My World series.

About the Photographers

Erwin and Peggy Bauer are among the world's most highly regarded wildlife photographers. Together the Bauers have published over twenty-five books and countless articles about their worldwide photographic expeditions.

The grizzly bears featured in this book were photographed in Denali National Park and Preserve (Alaska) and McNeil River Bear Sanctuary (Alaska).

Black bears were photographed in Glacier National Park (Montana), Yellowstone National Park (Wyoming), the northern Rocky Mountains (Montana), and the California Sierras.